RS   X

TAMES...
3
D1578281

/5/76

Books must be returned on or before
the latest date stamped below.

Class 821·91

No. J 593

Date	Date	Date	Date
27. APR. 1966	17. NOV. 1977		
25. NOV. 1967	14 FEB. 1980		
-8. APR. 1968	22. JUN. 1983		
29. MAY 1971			
25. OCT. 1971			
19. MAR. 1973			
16. OCT. 1974			
11. FEB. 1976			
29. APR. 1976			

BOOKSTORE
RETURN VIA BIB

WITHDRAWN FROM
TAMESIDE LIBRARIES

THE FERN ON THE ROCK

THE FERN ON THE ROCK

COLLECTED POEMS

1935 - 1965

BY

PAUL DEHN

HAMISH HAMILTON
LONDON

First published in Great Britain, 1965
by Hamish Hamilton Ltd
90 Great Russell Street London WC1
Copyright © 1965 by Paul Dehn

HYDE PUBLIC LIBRARIES				
VDR	Wills	DATE	'164	
PR	1·5|=	CAT.		
DEPT.	Alend	ST. × LAB.		
CLASS	821·91	CH.		
ACC. No.	J593	BRS.		

PRINTED IN GREAT BRITAIN BY
WESTERN PRINTING SERVICES LTD., BRISTOL

For those poems which have not already appeared in *The Day's Alarm*, *Romantic Landscape*, *Quake, Quake, Quake* (Hamish Hamilton) and *For Love and Money* (Reinhardt), acknowledgments are due to *The Listener*, *The New Statesman*, *Punch*, *Outposts*, Mr. Cyril Ray and Vista Books. 'Sirens' Song' won the Guinness Prize at the 1957 Cheltenham Festival.

To
ROGER MACHELL

CONTENTS

	page
Fern House, Kew	1
Lament for a Sailor	3
Bonfire	4
At the Dark Hour	5
Coming of Age	6
Habitué	7

Four Poems after Debussy

The Sunken Cathedral	11
Garden under the Rain	14
Sirens' Song	17
Poissons d'Or	22

Mourne Mountains	26
At the Buca di Bacco	29
Positano (1937)	30
Kamiros, Rhodes	31
Murano Glassblower	32
At Castelletto	33
The Swimmer	34
Trade	36
The Departed	37
Sea Change	38

The Shepherd and the Vine

The Bright Bird	40
The Riverbed	41
The Vine on the Hill	41

Ice on the Round Pond   43
London Summer   44
At my Window   46
Telegraph Poles   47
For a Sleeper   48
Circus Hand   49
In the Spring   50

Poems from the Film 'Waters of Time'

    Dawn Sequence   53
    Clock Sequence   55

Narcissus   58
Without any Warning   60
Willow-Warbler   62
In Time of Crisis   63
From a Valley   64
Balloon over Chelsea   65
Persons Unknown   66
The Sweet War Man is Dead   67
Killed in Action   68
Armistice   69
Aftermath   70
Anniversary   71
New Age   72
Explanation   74
Thirty-five   76

Danses Macabres

    Alternative Endings to an Unwritten Ballad   83
    A Game of Consequences   85
    Gutter Press   86
    Id   88

x

Who's for Tennyson?
  Blow 89
  Marijuanha in the Moated Grange 89
Epitaph for a Columnist 90
A Leaden Treasury of English Verse 91
Rhymes for a Modern Nursery 92
Weather Forecast 93
From a Modern Student's Song Book 94
From a Modern Hymnal 95

Three Poems by Jacques Prévert

Exercise Book 99
The Hurdy-Gurdy 101
How to Paint the Portrait of a Bird 103
Romantic Landscape 105

FERN HOUSE, KEW

Look! it is as though the sun,
Defrosting every spangled pane,
Should touch the fern engraven there
And turn it green again;
  Till the fronds, uncurling in
  The ice which held them captive, flow
  With water-music from the roof
  To tropic airs below;
And I, the boy who many a night
Fashioned in a jungle dream
The boat that I may never steer
Darkly against the stream,
  Quant the fathomed gangways, now,
  Brushed by all green things that grow.

Pondweed, here, without a pond
Wavers on the stagnant air,
Soft beside the trailing hand
Drifts the maidenhair
  And steeply to the lightless stream
  The tributary moonwort flows,
  Distilling on the river-bed
  A green light that glows.
Yet, by the cataract, how still
The prehistoric tendrils rise:
Antennae of enormous moth,
Spider with spores for eyes.
  Diluvian images, they stand
  Unstirring in an older land.

I

O yellow-hammered sun, my bird
In paradise beyond the cage,
Sing to the fossil mind, unscale
The lizard eye of age;
   Till fireflies, juggling in the dark
   Above the duckboard ripples, turn
   Candescent as the speckled light
   That filters through the fern;
And humming-birds in splendour thread
The tapestry a dreamer wove,
Slinging their scarlet shuttles through
The green warp of the grove.
   Now, behind the tall bamboo,
   Tiger lurks, and cockatoo.

The clock strikes one. A shadow falls
On serpent-stripe and tortoiseshell.
The toucan lifts his melon beak
In token of farewell;
   For waterfowl are calling on
   The English ornamental pool,
   Where carrot-coloured goldfish swim
   And the hot blood runs cool.
Close the door. Nor ever look
Behind you in the fronded pane.
Orpheus lost Eurydice,
But I must find again
   The little, star-crossed boy at play
   A continent of years away.

LAMENT FOR A SAILOR

Here, where the night is clear as sea-water
And stones are white and the sticks are spars,
Swims on a windless, mackerel tide
The dolphin moon in a shoal of stars.

Here, in the limbo, where moths are spinners
And clouds like hulls drift overhead,
Move we must for our colder comfort,
I the living and you the dead.

Each on our way, my ghost, my grayling,
You to the water, the land for me;
I am the fat-knuckled, noisy diver
But you are the quietest fish in the sea.

BONFIRE

Glows across Manresa Park
The altar-fire that no god sees,
Undedicated in the dark
Corinthian avenue of trees,

Beyond whose flaking colonnade
The smoke of sacrifice ascends
To a Greek moon from a green glade.
Here, by the wall, Arcadia ends.

The gods are fled without a cry
And the whole of history grieves,
Where the fluted dustbins lie
Like broken pillars in the leaves.

AT THE DARK HOUR

Our love was conceived in silence and must live
  silently.
This only our sorrow, and this until the end.
Listen, did we not lie all of one evening,
Your heart under my hand

And no word spoken, no, not even the sighing
Of pain made comfortable, not the heart's beat
Nor sound of urgency, but a fire dying
And the cold sheet?

The sailor goes home singing; the lamplit lovers
Make private movements in a public place.
Boys whistle under windows, and are answered;
But we must hold our peace.

Day, too, broke silently. Before the blackbird,
Before the trouble of traffic and the mist unrolled,
I shall remember at the dark hour turning to you
For comfort in the cold.

COMING OF AGE

Stare not at yourself when young,
The Ionian hair, the blue-john eye
That saw three ships go sailing by,
A starfish and a lizard's tongue.

Cry no more for yesterday,
The curved cheek, the carved hand
That traced a name across the sand
For a sea-wind to whisk away.

Quiet, now, are tops and rhymes;
The leaping shuttlecocks are still
And kites go down behind the hill
To meet the shadow as it climbs.

Now, from its most secret place,
Twitching at the white cocoon,
Crawls the Mind beneath the moon
To nibble at the puzzled Face.

HABITUÉ

Go home, go home, there is nothing for you here.
Already, now, beyond the cocktail-bar
In moss-green chairs, like crocuses appearing,
The pretty ones are pairing.
Touch the dove necktie, smooth the ebbing hair;
Stare,
Stare, if you must;
But call for hat and stick, before the tear
Lipping your pink and pug-dog eye
Proclaims a loneliness and lust
That no one, now, could wish to satisfy.

There is nothing for you here. Go home, go home
To the rococo mirror in your room
Where egg-shell beauty, as the mornings pass,
Has mottled in the glass.
Unstopper talc and turtle-oil and cream;
Dream,
Dream, if you will,
That once, crow's-feet ago, there was a time
When the fair sought you as now you seek the fair.
Tip the grave bar-boy. Pay the bill,
And walk alone under the evening air.

FOUR POEMS AFTER DEBUSSY

THE SUNKEN CATHEDRAL

Who knows, now, in what grey weather
The shoreline crumbled? Under what squall's whip
A mile of hooves
Smashed on the shingle, as the long combers
Leaped the last dyke and thundered over the flats
To the far sound of a bell?
And who remembers
How sheltered it was in the nave, singing together
By candlelight for the safety of a white ship
In peril on the sea?
                              Hang out your nets
To dry in the morning wind. No one believes,
Now, that it happened at all
And no one is left to tell.

No one is left to tell how Leviathan
Hurled his wet shoulder to the streaming wall,
And the west door
Went down like a gangway with a rattle of oak
On stone, as the sea surged luminously in.
It was all over so soon.
The surf broke
On the high altar. The figure of the Son of Man
Leaned slowly outward on His cross, and fell
In a swallowdive to the water. Then
The tide rose, and the top of the bell-tower
Vanished as silently as a
Sandcastle under the moon.

And under the moon in a shower of glass
Through windows open to the drifting weed
The first, small fishes
Glittered to the ground and turned to lunar dust.
So it began.
          The shelduck all night long
Crossed and re-crossed the sky;
At dawn the mist,
Lost on the water, looked for marram-grass
Among the swirling acres; and overhead
An alien world took wing—
Birds from the meadows and the marshes
Flocking all day above
The blown fields of the sea.

Beneath the sea came peace. The great bell still
Swung in the groundswell from a Gothic tower
Clappered with silence.
There was still movement: a scuttling under the pews,
A wriggle in a cranny, the malign
Flash of a cornered fin;
But, yet, no noise,
And with the centuries the fine sand fell
Through layers of mackerel-light to the dappled floor,
Sand over oak, sea against fretted stone,
Till time in a windless summer tipped the balance
Seaward, and the fishes
Took it for their own.

Today, when the cormorant in a shaft of light
Descends like a dark angel over the nave,
The mystery returns.
Lost among arches, where the lamps once

Shone in the vaulted shadow for their dead,
Glimmer the jellyfish;
And monuments
With limpet-lidded eyes lift fossil-white
Fingers in benediction. Full fathom five
The great cathedral lies on the ocean bed,
Its windows branching again with coral fern,
Spicule and starfish; its altar
With the green weed, awash.

The rest you have heard: how, in the bronze light
Of certain winter dawns too cold for wind,
It surfaces
With a sound like thunder and the water streaming
From windows open to the terrible sky.
Then, among iceberg-tall
Towers, chiming,
The cracked bells cry havoc and a white
Choir of gulls, not known on land,
Goes wailing among the aisles.
                    And silently
It founders again to the sheltered places,
Where substance is only shadow
And no one is left to tell.

II

GARDEN UNDER THE RAIN

The still rain drops; the raindrops still
Navigate my window-sill,
Where I watched them yesterday;
And still beyond the dripping eaves
By tanglewood and willow-leaves
The river bears the rain away.

From willow-tree to window-pane
Between the river and the rain
The garden's green asylum goes.
Here, the indecent toadstools sprout
And bryony that twists about
The thorny ropes of rambler rose.

Burdock, bindweed, barley-grass,
Razor-blade and broken glass
Constrict the worm that never dies.
Look! where maternal marrows sprawl,
The penitential raindrops fall
From chicory with wet blue eyes.

A flat, black boat, its bloat, fat back
Aground among the garden wrack
Lies where it has always lain,
Though yarrow-foam and sorrel-sand
Weave a slipway overland
To meet the river and the rain.

Though sorrel-sand and yarrow-foam
Call the stranded exile home,
The garden whispers: 'Peace! Be still.'
And still the river sings beyond
The seven catfish in the pond
Who may not wander where they will.

Another time, another day
(I sit and dream the rain away)
The wind sang, the sun shone.
O visionary weather-vane,
Point the west wind home again
And let the prisoners be gone.

Let convolvulus at dawn
Creep across a ghostly lawn
In flight from the captivity.
Shift the wind, unfix the star
Till the fever-swamps, that are,
Were not and will never be;

Till the boat in sunlight rides
With water slapping both its sides
On a noonday pleasure-cruise,
In the green shadow of whose wake
Voluptuary catfish take
Their dappled ease among the ooze.

Here, beyond my boyhood's eye,
Where salmon-coloured sandbanks lie,
The white birds whistle to the sea;

And fish and boat and bird are one,
Moving seaward in the sun.
O God of Gardens, set them free.

The still rain drops; the raindrops still
Navigate my window-sill,
Where I watched them yesterday;
And still beyond the dripping eaves
By tanglewood and willow-leaves
The river bears the rain away.

III

SIRENS' SONG

1.

It comes from below the horizon; and may be heard
On palmy days by sailors with cocked ear-rings
In the sea-heat of a summer without end:
Note after white note mounting on the skyline
Like a ladder of birds,
Till the entire chord
Towers overhead. And hearing
Voices but no words,
The landless see the land.

From grottos under coral towers
The foam erupts in fumaroles
And, drifting sideways in the wind,
Thins to a rainbow-spray and falls,
About the yellow cliff, in flowers.

Look, now! The rocks, from teeth on the horizon,
Loom tall as bergs; and though the blue-beaked lory,
Strutting the cabin-top, stops, blinks and recalls
Deep in the hinterland among the tendrils
The hot scream of a mate
Greener than poison,
The sailors feel only the glory
Of sound, and sand, and light
Whose dazzlement conceals

What jackals whining, each to each?
What vultures glaring, side by side,
At lemon-coloured jingle-shells
That lie in windrows on the beach
And tinkle with the laden tide?

Sooner or later, at the pull of the pale
Midday moon, these rocking shells will ring
One swimmer to the shore. Sooner or later
The fish will scatter, as the fingering wind
Strums on the shallows
In pursuit of all
These sounds, hither and thither winging,
That weave, now, like swallows
Across the waiting water.

Cry of whom, and call of what
(Uttered how, and echoed where?)
Whistle, flutter, wheel and chitter
Endlessly between the hot,
Hazy sea and heady air.

2.

Butēs, the son of Pandion, fairest of all
Mortal men, browner than sand or satin,
Halts on the Argo's prow with the salt spray stinging
His blue-spar eyes; hears the tumescent throb
(In its rib-shuttered room)
Of his heart's bacchanal,
And dives from the deck, brighter than beaten
Gold in the drifting spume
Towards the singing.

18

The jackals stiffen in their tracks,
The vultures freeze upon the tree.
The flesh is young, the day is long.
Something unearthly on the rocks
Yawns, and smiles, and slithers free.

The din of the deep water in his ear
Thins to a whisper; and the white sand, rearing
Steeply from the sea-bed, like a lover arches
Its ribs against his own.

                   Far, far astern
Falls the releasing silence.
Men at the masthead peer
Homeward. Only dead-still and staring
Back to the vanished islands,
The tethered lory perches.

    Take away the iron chain
    And on a green wing he would move,
    Shrieking, to a lost day
    When beak and claw were bright again
    And the groves were loud with love.

3.

Sooner or later those who have nothing to lose
But their own beauty, arrive at the desolate point
Of no return. They can only move forward,
The receding sun faint on a yellow shoulder
And the advancing night
Cold in their eyes.
After perfection, the descent.
After the sound of sand and light,
The dark drift shoreward,

Where fear ascribes the whitened bone
To non-existent goat and gull;
And what, for the evasive eye,
Was sea-wrack covering a stone
Is wet hair on a man's skull.

So Hylas on Argo, once, in the halcyon weather
Nearing his beauty's noon, awoke to the same
Soft, urgent voices calling from the land
As no-one might ever, in a later spring,
Have called to him again.
He went (he said) for water;
And the gulls still cry his name
Who ran beside the blue Aegean
To meet his boyhood's end.

Some believe that as he leaned
Panting by the pool alone,
Tendril-fingers drew him down.
But was the white and shuttling hand
Nymph's or naiad's, or his own?

And who calls Butēs, now, on the rocky height
Where huge as Atlas, seismic with desire,
Rutting into space over the rim of chaos
Past bawling planets and the deranged stars,
He couples with the Void:
Till the unhallowed light
Haloes with everlasting fire
The shrivelled thing that spills its blood
From no compassionate Cross.

The jackal and the vulture come
To feed upon his bones in peace;
And daintier teeth devour the heart,
While the Heroes carry home,
Immortally, the Golden Fleece.

IV

POISSONS D'OR

1.

God, I presume, observes it from
The ledges of eternity,
Uncovering a condor's eye
Vaster than the sun, yet lost
In the blue mileage of the sky:

Sirmio to the green southwest,
Mountain, lake and private wall,
Roof-tiles red as lobster-shell
And the dead composer's ghost
Attentive in a music room,

Where the living pianist
Conjures him for you and me
On whom the garden shadows fall
Beneath the pomegranate tree.
God, I assume, observes it all.

2.

But we, in the aquarian shade,
Can only make a minnow's guess,
Bumping our wits against the glass
That separates each filmy eye
From full, unfishy consciousness

Of what is high and what is dry.
We are the sort who only know
The water lily from below,
Darkly suspect divinity
In dragonflies beyond the weed,

And yet have seen a different sky
As the weed shifted with the wind
Until a nimbus hovered near
The jigsaw light upon the sand,
And a part of truth was clear.

3.

So now, at dusk, obedient to
The fingers of the pianist
And a dead composer's ghost,
These spectral goldfish, hanging fire,
Dart from a doorway and are lost.

Whick! The Veil-tail Blackamoor
Flirts a funeral fin and trails
Her trinket-golden belly scales
Skyward to the evening star;
And red Orandas wriggle through

The vine-leaves at the villa door
To vanish in an olive grove
Where, white among the nightingales,
The mooning Eggfish gently wave
The butterflies that are their tails.

4

Starlight, water-music fall
About us in a sequin shower;
Each vermilion dragonflower
Upon the pomegranate tree,
Responsive to the lotus hour,

Lifts a fin and flickers free:
Free as the Comet-fish to thread
The constellations overhead
And flash imperially by
The obsolete Celestial

Ballooning slowly up the sky;
Free as the golden and the red,
The spotted and the Chinese white,
Who heard the music of the dead
And leaped from lacquer into light.

5.

How can we say they do not live,
These glitter-ghostly shoals who keep
Unwinking vigil in the deep
Rock-canyons of the human mind,
And may not stir, yet may not sleep,

Till the weed, shifting in the wind,
Permits a needle ray of light
To taper from the fiery height
And touch one swimmer with its wand?
How can we say they do not move

Who, now, like meteors ascend
From nowhere into sudden view
And gild the soft Italian night
And stay there, tumbling in the blue,
Till music and the twilight end?

———————

MOURNE MOUNTAINS

In the dandelion light, in the bright
Halo that falls on the hills
At the end of a watery day;
When the rook rides by
Like a witch on the wind,
And the rain
Hangs in rats'-tails, out and away
Over Dundrum Bay;

    Lay, my love, your ear to the
    Cold shell of the twilight. Hear
    The sound of the Shimna
    Far and clear as it flows
    Deep under ledge,
    Rockpool, ridge,
    Sedge and the sycamore tree
    To the desolate sea.

Eastward, the grey
Hulk of a cloud
Crawls over the crest and
Sprawls on the saddleback, slack
As a feeding slug;
Crepuscular things
Clap their wings in the wood, and the cleg
Goes mooning about on a blood-binge over the bog.

    But lift, my love, your eyes to the
    West, where still

The light falls clean
On a green hill over the wall;
Where the far-off
House, the horse and the hen
Are sea-shell white in the grass
And the ragwort flickers its small,
Coastal light
To the sheep that pass.

Sleep; as the night
Sails over the land, and moors
In a fathom of stars
At the sounding's end.
Yours be the haze on the
Light-buoy moon; but mine
To beware of the weather, awake
To the gathering gale at the
Head of the ghyll,
Where the power of darkness, riding high,
Moves in for the kill.

Look! on the mountain top,
My dreamer,
The wind is amok—
A horned and battering ram
In the afterglow.
The boulder dam
Bursts on the height; and slow
As a sea let go,
The mist breaks over the crest
And falls like
Falls to the fields below.

Here, in the spindrift air,
Mysterious wheat
Swirls at my feet like
Foam, who stand
Where land is no longer land
But the white scurr
Of a squall at sea;
Where the speedboat hull of the hills
Heels in the wind, and the rain
Smacks like a bow-wave
Over the bowsprit-spur.

Dream, in the undertow.
Here is my heart
By one day's weather made new,
Washed in the wind and the rain
With a love so deep
That you,
Even in sleep, may know.

AT THE BUCA DI BACCO

Over and over, to-night,
The pianist plays by the reef
In the sea-green light
Of lamp under leaf.
His fingers are fish,
Leaping
The surf of a glimmering keyboard;
And over and over the drummer is keeping
Time, with the swing and the swish
Of waves on the seaboard.

Over and over the moon,
Drifting from key to key,
Fingers an endless tune
Of light on the sea;
Whose virginal air,
Meeting
The sensuous air of the summer,
Sounds over and over to breakers beating
Time, with the whisk and the whirr
Of a lazy drummer.

POSITANO (1937)

Beyond the mountainside,
The stars wink like a village; and this steep
Village itself is stars, whose pin-points glow
Faint from their firmament of rock. Below,

Hanging a fathom deep,
Fishermen's lamps are lunar on the tide;
And out to sea the trail of the risen moon
Is pools of light in the wake of a skimming stone.

KAMIROS, RHODES

This old man, with eroded skin
And blue, mosaic eyes alert
To the young sprigs who pass him by,
Carries a bunch of wild-thyme in
The pocket of his veteran shirt;
And sniffs his salad days. So I

Shall wear this island in my mind
And see again in calmer years
Aleppo pines above the shore
Lean on a recollected wind
That still may sting the eye to tears,
When thyme and tide are wild no more.

MURANO GLASSBLOWER

The flutter-thundered furnace hums
Its omens to the waiting air.
The Master licks majestic thumbs
And twists an incandescent mess
Of nebular, galactic glass
Into a fireball on a rod.
The boy-apprentice hovers near—
Dark angel articled to God.

God lifts the trumpet to his mouth.
The fireball reddens to a sun;
And east and west and north and south
The skeins and veins of colour probe
The cooling surface of a globe
Needled with green, and threaded blue,
Cinnamon-stranded, serpent-spun,
Pupilled with every tribal hue.

The attentive angel wipes God's brow.
Obstetric instruments are brought.
Snip, snip! The world's cut free. And now
Master and novice move away,
Not waiting for the seventh-day
Hosannas that we sinners sing
In praise of this divinely wrought
And suddenly quite vulgar thing.

AT CASTELLETTO

Here by the shore where the young trout, leaping,
Stipple the lake like a shower of rain,
And three boats bleach on a high-dry mooring,
A goat-boy swings from the mainmast rope,
Dark as a clapper in the sunlight soaring
Skyward, and swooping
Down again.

And stroke for stroke (as the child swings
Into the light, where life began)
A church-bell tolls from the mountainside:
Watch, watch the air between
The boy, who flies in the heat of the sun,
And the bell that rings
For a cold man.

Watch, watch the narrowing air
Between the sun and the dark storm,
The killer kite and the glittering fish.
Here is the pact, immune to prayer,
Of the first wish and the last fact,
The brown bright flesh
And the mealy worm.

Ding, dong! The frontiers narrow,
The wind thickens, the grasses bend,
The kite drops like a dark arrow—
Sunlight, fish-light, all are lost
And the boy, who swings from a tall mast,
Is a dead man
At a rope's end.

33

THE SWIMMER

Windhover, gliding
On the blue firmament
Of noonday water,
  I ride at ease
And see below me
Fathomed in twilight
Primeval mountains
  Under seas.

Barnacle-snowcapped,
Their peaks, sliding
Beneath the wing-tip
  Which is my hand,
Shadow the gorge
And the dark weed stirring
Its forest fleece in a
  Tidal wind.

So God, dividing
The light from the darkness,
Moved on the face of
  Earlier seas
And called forth creatures
From every crater,
Where once erupted
  Anemones:

The great eel
As long as a valley,
The lunar crab
  On a hill's brow,
Squid with the cataract
Tentacles tumbling
Waterfall-white to the
  Rocks below.

Then who dare fathom
This land's mystery
With no lodestar
  To bear him light
But a constellation
Of sunstruck fishes
Falling in fragments
  Through the night?

TRADE

I was the shingle-kicker,
The cocky, the worldly-wise,
The trim talker, the easy walker,
The boy with the money-box eyes.

Turn, turn in your bed;
For whom the days were golden,
That now are dead.

I am the longshore swaggerer,
The teller of ten-o'clock lies,
The beer-swiller, the Card, the Killer,
The man with the money-bag eyes.

Drink, drink and be strong;
For whom the nights were nimble,
That now are long.

THE DEPARTED

Under a cliff-top wind, the grass
   Foams at the foot of pierstake pines;
   And out to sea the same wind whines
In halyards of the ships that pass.

White in your wake the waters lie,
   Who leave these daisy-laden shores,
   And which is foam and which are flowers
I cannot tell with mortal eye.

But where the future meets the past
   And there is neither land nor sea
The pine that yet shall be a mast
   Sings to the mast that was a tree.

SEA CHANGE

From the Round Pond this February morning
I hear the outboard flutter of wings on the water
And a sea-mew's siren.

Look where this grey gull, in the sunlight turning,
Circles the mainland and skims into harbour
Like a Catalina.

Ducks at the dockside, their brown hulls bobbing,
Cluster of masted swans, the longshore sparrows,
Swarm on the tide-line.

Only this early boy, at my dream's ebbing,
Thrusting his white-winged yacht among the waders,
Scatters a seascape.

THE SHEPHERD
AND THE VINE

A Song Cycle
For Peter Pears and Julian Bream

All day, below the turning sky
Where bird and bee at random pass,
A sheep's cold and captive eye
Is fixed upon the grass.

But mine is free in a man's head
To fix or follow, as it will,
The bright bird, the riverbed
And the vine on the hill.

Then who, below the turning sky,
Is happier? The sheep or I?

THE BRIGHT BIRD

At dawn beneath the risen sun
The lizard scuttles to a stone,
The wren rings in the hazelwood,
The butterfly assaults the bud
And the great bee drones till noon;

When none but little insects hum,
The bud lies all alone,
The hazelwood is dumb, dumb,
And empty, the stone.

Still, on a briar, the Red-Backed Shrike
Stands sentinel above the corn.
His mask is black. His butcher-beak
Was made to break and spike and hook
His victim on a thorn.

And look! below the burning sky,
Crucified on a tree:
The lizard and the butterfly,
The wren and the bee.

40

THE RIVERBED

Run, river, run
Into this cave
From the heat of the sun
To the cold of the grave.

Say farewell
To the peace you had,
And in a narrow hell
Go secretly mad.

Nor fish nor moss
May follow you, where
The bats hiss
In the vaulted air;

But the far sigh,
The deep groan
And the loud cry
Are the river's own.

THE VINE ON THE HILL

(*It is said that young wine clouds in the cask when the vine from which it came is in flower.*)

All winter the young wine,
That I would drink tonight,
Lay captive in the cask
And amber-bright;

Clear, unclouded
And amber-bright, until
Its own vine in April
Flowered on the hill.

O how can a flower,
On a hill apart,
Cloud what should lighten
My troubled heart,

That knew no trouble
All winter, until
My own love in April
Flowered on the hill?

Now, in the long night
I wake my thirst away,
Counting the sheep
As I have done all day.

All day, below the turning sky
Where bird and bee at random pass,
A sheep's cold and captive eye
Is fixed upon the grass.

But mine is free in a man's head
To fix or follow, as it will,
The bright bird, the riverbed
And the vine on the hill.

Then who, below the turning sky,
Is happier? The sheep or I?

ICE ON THE ROUND POND

This was a dog's day, when the land
Lay black and white as a Dalmatian
And kite chased terrier kite
In a Kerry Blue sky.

This was a boy's day, when the wind
Cut tracks in the sky on skates
And noon leaned over like a snowman
To melt in the sun.

This was a poet's day, when the mind
Lay paper-white in a winter's peace
And watched the printed bird-tracks
Turn into words.

LONDON SUMMER

My window lays its grid on the map of a sky
Charted with molten islands; and the sun
Sails mythically into the towered west
Till London is Athens, Valparaiso, Rome.
Steeple and dome,
Which, in the heat of noon,
Wavered as though submerged, float on the last
Sea-green tide of a day's end, and die.

Now the weaving lights appear
From pavement, tree and parapet
Till the drowsy eyes forget
Which, in the Sicilian air,
Is firefly, star and cigarette.

Browner than bracken, the barefoot corner-boys
Lean over green grapes bubbling on a barrow
And watermelons, plucked where the whip-poor-will
Whined all night like a hawker about my home.
Summer has come
And will be here tomorrow
With litter of peel and popcorn, when the still
Sidewalk is brushed again by the morning breeze.

A Neon moon over World's End
Is nightfall's first advertisement;
The ripples on the waterfront
Lower their Venetian blind;
The sparrow ceases argument.

Only on the left bank of the east river
(The Liffey, at sunrise, with its paintbox houses;
At night, the Grand Canal whose swans explore
The dark, like gondolas) I hear the shrill
Bat-call
Chatter of young voices
Swarming to the shaft of light at a bar door,
To the honky-tonky piano and the blue-jeaned lover.

Welter-weight and matelot,
Ganymede and grenadier
See, beyond the rendezvous,
Life forever amber through
Half a pint of bitter beer.

This City is all cities under the wicked moon,
While summer lasts. Here the Embankment glimmers,
A lemon-grove of lights, at the edge of all
Waters in history; and we, who share
The fabled air
That is a London summer's,
Stretch in a dream our seven-leagued limbs and stroll
A stateless world, where none are alien.

But O what fancy shall defy
The nightmare ague in the bone
When, beneath a winter sky,
The lost, unearthly cities lie
Cold and separate as stone?

AT MY WINDOW

Being alone this morning, I surmise
You found elsewhere to go, yesterday night,
Or just forgot.

A criss-cross gull in grey, distracted flight
Quarters the empty sky, and cries and cries,
As I must not.

TELEGRAPH POLES

These, in the dusk, are bars
  On the lit score of spring,
When early-comer stars
  Lean outward, listening.

Rams to the music muster
  Their horned and tenor herds
Where, on a wire stave, cluster
  The semi-quaver birds

FOR A SLEEPER

Minute-hand and moon and mind,
Turning in a windless night,
Gather moment as the light
Halts before your window-blind.

Over clockface, field and farm,
Narrows the sector of the dark
Till springing into light, a lark
Touches-off the day's alarm.

CIRCUS HAND

All my life long
  Since I was thirteen,
Loved like St. Francis
  Is what I would have been.

The fish still scatter,
  The pony shies,
The snake bites
  And the bird flies

Yet here is one who is
  What I would have been
All my life long;
  And he is thirteen.

IN THE SPRING

Now, when the wind dies easily
At half-past five across the Square
And chimney-cowls like little owls
Blink in the turning air;
When the early blossoms lie
Japanned against the evening sky,
And what is young seems fair:

Bear with me, beloved,
You as young as Spring,
If I fear to lose you;
I, who, to please you,
Would give any thing.

Dusk will hide deficiencies,
The dark is kind to skin and bone.
Conjure back all that I lack
And let us lie alone,
Till the sifted stars are sent
Spinning down the firmament,
And the seed is sown.

Soon, soon, beloved,
The sun will mock my pride
Tomorrow I may lose you;
I, who, to please you,
Would even stand aside.

Poems from the Film
'WATERS OF TIME'

1. DAWN SEQUENCE

Yesterday, the ships were carried up-river
On the great conveyor-belt of the flood tide,
Which drummed between Thanet and the Tower of
    London
To the whine of the wind and the squeaking of gulls,

But slackened at sundown, far above harbour,
Halting at last in the higher reaches
By Richmond, quiet under the fading stars.

And still, at daybreak, the slack water
Sleeps and is empty of all movement
Save a white regatta of swans, who skirmish
Back and forth like yachts on a start-line,
Awaiting the boom of the morning gun.

(*Big Ben chimes*)

Look, where the risen sun explodes in the windows,
Striking at spandril, bead and spindle,
Battlement, parapet, buttress after buttress
Held at the slope like a line of bayonets

And towering above his tented army of rooftops,
The great and glittering helmet of Paul.
God looks down on the waking river.

(*Dissolve to Neptune-figurehead, Gravesend*)

And a god looks back, who was king of the sea;
At the touch of whose trident, this flat water
Grew curly as the ocean in old maps
With porpoise rolling in the light of morning
And dolphins slapped by the cherubim winds.

The salt-sea fishes have gone to their grave's end.
Only, far up, in the river god's kingdom,
Under the reeds where the Thames runs softly,
A pike yawns in the Putney shallows,
An eel opens a watery eye.

The river-fish wake in the manner of men;
And Man wakes with them, the poor Fish . . .

(The dockers go to work)

II. CLOCK SEQUENCE

Yesterday the longitude of ships on the main-deep,
The pluck and the knock of Leviathan tides
Were measured for the mariner on fine chronometers
Like this, by Harrison of Barrow-upon-Humber
A Yorkshire carpenter of yeoman stock. . . .

Tick, tock, tick, tock

Yesterday the towers were trees on the skyline.
Poplar and Royal Oak, Nine Elms, Barn Elms,
One Tree, Plumstead and sadler's willows
Swayed in the wind that blew from the mudflats
By Lambeth Marsh and the Meadows at Westminster.

The trees are dead, but the names stick. . . .

Tock, tick, tock

The swans lead, where the sailboat follows,
And sailboats follow in a steamer's wake.
Web-foot, centre-board, paddlewheel, propeller
Have moved on the surface of London's river
Whose wash, at their passing, is light as the windflaw
That moves on the face of the waters of Time.

And still, in the winter, the air is heavy
With sweet smell of malt, the tang of tobacco
And the sleepy fragrance from wharf and warehouse

Of summer harvest and autumn vintage,
Wine in the wood, and the ten spices:

> Nutmeg, ginger, cloves, red capsicum,
> Cassia, chillies, grain of paradise,
> Pepper, pimento, cinnamon quills. . . .

Hampstead was a hill on the far horizon
Where ploughboys, walking under a wide sky,
Could whistle down-wind to the distant City,
To ships under sail, and the sail of a windmill
Turning in the shadow of Old St. Paul's.

And Londoners, waiting by the river-stairheads
At Cuckold's Point, Shadwell, Watergate and Wapping,
Could whistle-up wherries, whose watermen cried:
'Eastward Ho!' 'Westward ho!' 'Whither would you
  journey?'

And still the seagulls whistle to the watermen
From Gallions Reach to the Lower Pool.
The collier leads where the wherry-boat follows,
And wherry-boats sail in the wake of swans.

(To the Crescent wine vaults)

Roll out the barrels from Spain and from Portugal,
Pipes, butts, hogsheads, quarter-casks, octaves,
Fino, Amontillado, Oloroso, Manzanilla,
Quinta da Roriz, Tua, Boa Vista,
Tawny in the cask as the sun in November,
To be drunk with a neck of pork roasted in
  gooseberries,
Meat pie, pudding and Wensleydale cheese!

56

Roll them to London, O bountiful billows,
In firkin and kilderkin, see where they come!
Shipped by Fonseca, Ferreira, de Soto,
Cockburn, Sandeman, Campbell and Menzies,
Belly-fat barrels, rotund as an alderman,
Rumbling to rest like a big bass drum.

. . . And rest in peace in the vaults under London,
In a Dead City of seven-mile alleys,
Gaslit, windless, save for the wash of air
Fluttering the fungus as a barrel passes—
Batswing-fungus, born of the wine fumes,
Fed on a surfeit of Port and Sherry,
Till the yawning roof of the vault resembles
The roof of an ogre's mouth, the morning after.

Rest in peace till your day of judgment
By plump connoisseurs at Livery banquets,
Pear-shaped Dons in a candle-lit Common Room,
Lord Lieutenants with lambent faces
And florid ladies in Four Ale bars.

Sunshine of Spain and sunshine of Portugal,
Brought by boat to the Port of London,
From grape to barrel, from barrel to hold,
From hold to deck and from deck to dock. . . .

Tick, tock, tick, tock . . . (to a fade)

———————

NARCISSUS

By the black watch-face of this mica water
Where lilies, burning blue at the dial's rim,
Number night's flattering hours;
Where the cicada marks each clicking minute
And clockwork frogs croak for the passing quarter;
Here, where an owl's whistle
Warns like a distant hooter;
Tall in the mist behind me towers
Time with his cold chisel.

To-morrow the golden clapper of the sun
Shall swing to the zenith, strike from a hollow sky
The din of noon, and burnish
My pool to a mirror's brightness. O Narcissus,
Are you—the summer boy—this tired man
Whose hot, imploring eyes
Seek the consent in mine
For those swift delicacies that banish
Desire, as the dew dries?

Are you—slow victim to your quiver's arrow,
Whose beauty fought with death—this grained face
Touched-up by no neat hand,
Focused too finely in a lens leaf-shuttered?
Lord, let there be a little rain, to furrow
The pool's face and scatter
My image on the morrow.
Let there be but a little wind
To ruffle this water.

Only to-night, under the galleried stars,
Spot-lit by no long moonbeam, let me lie
Close to the cold glass
Where in the dark, twin brother, you are young
And I as young as you. Now nothing stirs
Save Time, whose itching thumbs
Snuff-out the guttering hours.
A dawn wind hisses in the grass
And the black sunlight comes.

WITHOUT ANY WARNING

Listen, I have heard him chuckle in derelict places,
Known panic and the fisted fear that knocks
By marsh, moor and grey meadow;
And I have heard
A catspaw wind behind me pounce, pursue and pass,
Have seen the grass
Flat as a frightened bird
And water, blown sideways, a veiled widow.
Not from tall tower, no, nor your high houses
Rocking suddenly over a hill's brink
Falls the shadow.

But especially wet and walking on rainy afternoons,
Out of the mist a mountain, out of the mountain
    laughter,
A light unlooked-for, a cloud curling;
And I have known
Small tadpole-terrors nibble at my knees,
Have heard flat seas
Lie sucking at a stone,
Shifting of shingle and a conch calling
Across the sand that snickers in the dunes
To where one seagull, like a spark in the sunset
Tossed up, is falling.

Look, your great goat's-foot from the sky descending
And lean beard blown streaming off the hills!
Pan, Pan, I have watched awaken

60

Beyond the cavern's roof
Leaves like larks flocking on the upturned wind,
Have seen the land
Leap to the skidding hoof
And Earth's desire spent in the hissing bracken.
Yet, in your wake, such stillness without ending
As only moth or owl on mouse-manoeuvres
Shall ever quicken.

WILLOW-WARBLER

In boyhood, as was fitting,
I first saw and heard
(Low-fluting, quick-flitting)
This small, restless bird

Who made our spring seem brief,
Blown by a migrant breeze
To land like a green leaf
On the still-budding trees.

Now, faded in the fall,
It clings to a bare tree,
Awaiting the wind's call
And the call of the sea.

IN TIME OF CRISIS

As though through glass I watch the waters of evening
Fill the green air, and homing birds
Rise in a skein of bubbles to the west.

Late in the aquarium light a shoal of children,
Sensing far off the fall of darkness,
Scatters like a school of fishes and is lost.

But I keep vigil; separate as the swifts
Who scull about the sky's surface
And watch the last light gather, and may not rest.

FROM A VALLEY

High overhead the marksman hawk,
Sharpshooting in the pass,
Sees plover, snipe and pipit burst
Like buckshot from the grass.

The catapulted curlews dive,
Lamenting as they go,
Down the great quadrant of the wind
To a world's end below.

But quiet men of middle-earth
Moon homeward, unaware
Of how the black formations mass
In windy middle-air.

Across this tapestry of trees
The fading sunlight steals
And wagtails glide about the lawn
As though on little wheels.

BALLOON OVER CHELSEA

Pavilioned evening covers all.
The ropes are cut, the people cry,
And like a quilted tennis ball
It bounces slowly to the sky;

Sails out across the City park,
The sooty Thames, the setting sun.
Look! in the truce before the dark
The twilight is Victorian.

PERSONS UNKNOWN

Time for tea. I listened, with eyes lifted
To the winter hills, the bells, the sound of a gun;
And still the mist, like steam from a kettle, drifted
Over the hot-plate sun.

What have they killed out there on the cold soil
Counties, countries away? I cannot see;
For the mist lies thick between me and the passing
    bell,
And the bell says: Time for tea.

THE SWEET WAR MAN IS DEAD

The sweet war man is dead and
rotten; sweet chucks, beat not
the bones of the buried. When
he breathed, he was a man.
                    Love's Labour's Lost, V, ii.

Their stricken bones lie all about the world,
Who were my friends in England; and the law
Permits me to have loved them, who lack flesh.

Eyes winked, once, in the skull. Ribs that are curled
Under the sand, under the sea, under the hairy paw
Of Death who sent the flies, who sent the fish,

Had once a heart. Pluck me that heart, now,
From bird's beak, eel-gut and the maggot's mouth;
Put back those eyes, where the eternal tide

Sings in the sockets; on the crackpot brow
Pencil the leaf-light shadow-lines of youth;
For these bare bones were children, when they died.

So must I mourn among the glutted gulls,
Cry to a shark, weep with the fat, white worm
Who turns and nods to me across the stones.

They feasted and are full. Only these skulls
Ring emptily and need no requiem,
Being at peace. Lie easy, now, poor bones.

KILLED IN ACTION

We seek the same prey, Scavenger,
With hooked and lonely hands.
To-night at your long table
Sit six of my friends.

Under the star-shells
Glisten and decay
The six grave faces
I loved as a boy.

Yours, now, that once were mine,
Rib, wrist and hair.
Is there at your long table,
Prince, an empty chair?

ARMISTICE

It is finished. The enormous dust-cloud over
   Europe
Lifts like a million swallows; and a light,
Drifting in craters, touches the quiet dead.

Now, at the bugle's hour, before the blood
Cakes in a clean wind on their marble faces,
Making them monuments; before the sun,

Hung like a medal on the smoky noon,
Whitens the bone that feeds the earth; before
Wheat-ear springs green, again, in the green spring

And they are bread in the bodies of the young:
Be strong to remember how the bread died,
   screaming;
Gangrene was corn, and monuments went mad.

AFTERMATH

On the far side of the weather were toy yachts
Jinking in a park-breeze; were the streets
Flustered by prams; and kites
Cartwheeling under a swept sky.

This side, and above me, was the bombed spire
Latticed with silence; was the queer hour
Of a stopped clock, and the chair
Scraped to a sun-trap over cold stone.

The young are broad awake. But I, where the
    wind shifts,
Under the spire, under the sun-shafts,
Still drowse; and between us drifts
The thinning curtain of this unshared spring.

ANNIVERSARY

This was our earliest walk together
Who seven years later stood
Loving each other equally
Under the same April weather
And the wild cherry like the ghost of a tree
Come back to haunt the wood.

NEW AGE

To-night the wind comes screaming up the road
Like a train in the tube. Over my cringing head
Gas-lamps are ghosts of the still-marching dead
Whose butchered eyes, blown open,
Pity our cold condition.
Here, in this rotting air,
The traffic lights ripen
From green to yellow, from yellow to red;
And I, with a cobweb of rain in my hair,
Trudge between tram-lines, seeking a world's
    salvation.

Only the lost are with me, only the late
And the last, lonely stragglers in the street:
A drunkard in the lamplight, on whose coat
Something still glistens;
The frosted whore who marks
My footfall on the stone,
Sniffs in the wind and listens
Under the red lamp of the traffic light;
And a flash boy, adrift in the pin-stripe rain,
Edging towards the privacy of parks.

These, my cold company; whose nailed feet
Scrape on the pavements of eternal night;
The down-at-heel, who drift in the wet light,
Seeking a wind to blow
The spent leaf from its stalk;

Who long for death,
As the leaf longs for snow.
These only are unafraid, who throng to meet
The wind that bears a world's end in its breath.
O Christ, have pity on them, where they walk.

Raise Your nailed hand! Unwedge the window-frame
Of the sleek man in bed. Shiver the dream
That muffles his drugged ear to the crack of doom
And let him hear the shriek
Of the relentless wind
And the loose casement, rattling.
Listen. The clocks strike,
Heard by the lost; unheard in the locked room
Under the sheet where the sly hands go shuttling
This night and evermore, world without end.

EXPLANATION

When the pillars of smoke, that towered between
    heaven and earth
On the day we died, have thinned in the wind and
    drifted
And the hooded crow flaps home across the volcanic
    sky,
Somewhere beyond and below the littered horizon
(Out of the cave into the cold air)
Man, I suppose, will emerge and grow wise and read
What we have written in guilt, again with an innocent
    eye.

Then, if the desperate song we sang like storm-cocks
At the first flash, survives the ultimate thunder
To be dreamily misunderstood by the children of
    quieter men,
Remember that we who lived in the creeping shadow
(Dark over woodland, cloud and water)
Looked upon beauty often as though for the last time
And loved all things the more, that might never be
    seen again;

Who chewed the leaf, uncertain of seeing the hawthorn
Scatter its stars the length of a lane in summer,
Or fingered the sparrow's egg that might never be
    born a bird;
And wondered, even, whether the windflaw moving
Silently over the water's surface

Should gain the distant edge of the lake in safety
Before the inferno struck, whose echoes shall never be
   heard.

I sing to a child unborn, begotten in guilt
By us who have made the world unfit for his coming.
Our only comfort: that Christ was born in the cold.
I know, I know that a legion of singers before us
Looked their last on much that was lovely
And perished as we must perish. But who will
   remember
That most of them wept and died only because they
   were old?

THIRTY-FIVE

On the middle night of my life, a north wind lifted
The tarpaulin of the forest and ranged southward
Trailing its tatters over Whaley Moor.
Now, in the leafless silence,
Winter came quietly. The cold light drifted
Down through my cage of trees, beyond whose bare
Branches I saw the sun's last brilliance
Lose grip on ledge, on moleskin moss, on stone,
To slip, like the years, away; and at my back
Swung from its open grave on Black Rock
The white, atrocious moon.

Caged between moon and sun, dead world and dying,
Between two deaths on the middle night of my life,
I saw Earth's crust split and disintegrate
Behind an iron cloud
And all my green years lost, with the sparks flying
Like a kicked bonfire over the field of night.
They flared in the Western furnaces, and died:
History and self; plain upon storied plain,
The marching dynasties; and a boy's blazer,
Bell, book and candlelight, wineglass and razor,
Bayonet, blood and bone.

In the end and the beginning was the Word
Which made and shall unmake all. But not until now
On the middle night of my life at the dead moon's rising,
Not since the voice of One

Moved on the bucking waters like a bird,
Dividing light from darkness, improvising
Star, mayfly, wood-anemone and Man,
Has Man been driven to measure his own time
On Earth against the days of Earth itself;
Or, scanning the finite and the infinite gulf,
Feared them to be the same.

This our new terror, by me to be remembered
Here in the limbo dividing light from darkness,
Feeling the tidal pull of the dead moon
On the middle night of my life;
That the days of the world, once countless, shall be
    numbered
As Man's are numbered threescore and years ten.
Of the two stories, ending, both are brief;
For the rib and the rock shall crack in the lunar
    weather
On these flint hills where Earth and I grow older,
Bough break like bone, the stream and the blood run colder
Which yet may freeze together.

And men shall die, knowing a new grief:
That the world may die, in which their works should live,
Making the life void and the works vain;
As I know now, who stand
Under bare trees on the middle night of my life
With the white moonlight worming at my brain
And the shadow of Black Rock across the land.
Mankind shall weep upon the latter day,
Under the mushroom cloud, not for their own
Death; but because their children and their town
Died the same night as they.

The last cloud set with the sun. A wind's blade
Struck sparks from the turning wheel of the night
    sky.
Now, through the bars of my uncovered cage,
The first inquisitive stars
Looked down like children's eyes, and multiplied:
Till, on the middle night of my life, an age
Of grief and terror lifted; till the years,
Drifting in sparks on the back of the north wind,
Joined the high galaxies. The stars looked down
Like children's eyes; and such a peace was mine
As children understand.

Something a man must love, or a World ends.
Too many have murdered in the cause of Love
Who wrongly loved and therefore wrongly died.
Let there be one belief,
Loved of all men, whose furtherance depends
Only on love; and men will pray aloud
(As I do, now, on the middle night of my life)
Lashing their bodies to the pitching spar
Of peace; lest, like Ulysses, they should see
Perilous islands, and be tempted by
The siren song of war.

Take arms no longer in the cause of God;
For, in the life hereafter, shall Mahomet
Spit on the cross of Calvary, or Siva
The decalogue deny?
Divinity is numberless, and good
Only as prophets are good. God is a river
To whom all gods are tributary; and I
Seek the main stream on the middle night of my life

Knowing that, even in death, I shall not ride
The confluence of waters. Sheathe your blade.
Let there be one belief.

Son of the skeleton who was my friend,
Seed of his clean-picked loin! Take arms no more
In hope to make the Earth a greener place
That children may inherit.
From this night forward, arms shall be the end
Of man and the children of men. A boy's face
Shall blacken with his father's. The poor spirit
That gave one child a song to sing must die,
On the middle night of my life, for the want of a child
To sing it. There shall be, in the lunar world,
No more posterity.

Love then and believe in the child who, this day, runs
But who shall read to-morrow. Love and believe
In the spinner of tops, who yet shall spin your twilight
Into his daring day.
How can we murder these, who have yet no sins,
No hatreds and no languages? The skylight
Over the nursery world, where children cry
For need of another morning, shall not splinter
At the flinging of a final stone; and I,
On the middle night of my life, may fitlier pray
That spring will follow winter.

Winter came quietly, spreading its dust sheet
White over field and farm. (This tree, this town
Will not be needed, now, until the spring.)
Dead moon and dying sun
Were knockers in hell's gate; but the infant light

Of innumerable stars, beyond them beckoning,
Signalled the way to peace. A child is born.
One love brings stars about us. One belief
Shall lift mankind among the firework skies,
Till all and I look out with children's eyes
On the middle night of my life.

DANSES MACABRES

ALTERNATIVE ENDINGS TO AN
UNWRITTEN BALLAD

I stole through the dungeons, while everyone slept,
   Till I came to the cage where the Monster was kept.
There, locked in the arms of a Giant Baboon,
   Rigid and smiling, lay . . . MRS. RAVOON!

      *   *   *

I climbed the clock-tower in the first morning sun
   And 'twas midday at least ere my journey was done;
But the clock never sounded the last stroke of noon,
   For there, from the clapper, swung MRS. RAVOON.

      *   *   *

I hauled in the line, and I took my first look
   At the half-eaten horror that hung from the hook.
I had dragged from the depths of the limpid lagoon
   The luminous body of MRS. RAVOON.

      *   *   *

I fled in the tempest, through lightning and thunder,
   And there, as a flash split the darkness asunder,
Chewing a rat's-tail and mumbling a rune,
   Mad in the moat squatted MRS. RAVOON.

      *   *   *

I stood by the waters so green and so thick,
   And I stirred at the scum with my old, withered stick;
When there rose through the ooze, like a monstrous
     balloon,
   The bloated cadaver of MRS. RAVOON.

      *   *   *

Facing the fens, I looked back from the shore
Where all had been empty a moment before;
And there, by the light of the Lincolnshire moon,
Immense on the marshes, stood . . . MRS. RAVOON!

Footnote : The Lady survives, though Anthony Asquith tried to liquidate
her on October 5th, 1955, in a postlude:

'Free at Last!'—and I smiled as HER Requiem soared
Through the incense and sank to a soft final chord;
When, harsh and obscene like a bestial bassoon,
From the crypt rose the laughter of . . . MRS. RAVOON!

A GAME OF CONSEQUENCES

Coffee-cups cool on the Vicar's harmonium,
  Clever guests giggle and duffers despond.
Soft as the patter of mouse-feet, the whisper
  Of Eversharp Pencil on Basildon Bond.

Separate hands scribble separate phrases—
  Innocent, each, as the new-driven snow.
What will they spell, when the paper's unfolded?
  Lucifer, only, and Belial know.

'Ready, Miss Montague? Come, Mr. Jellaby!'
  (Peek at your papers and finger your chins)
'Shy, Mr. Pomfret? You'd rather the Vicar . . . ?
  Oh, good for the Vicar!' The Vicar begins:

'FAT MR. POMFRET met FROWSTY MISS
    MONTAGUE
  Under the BACK SEAT IN JELLABY'S CART.
He said to her: WILL YOU DO WHAT I
    WANT YOU TO?
  She said to him: THERE'S A SONG IN
    MY HEART.'

What was the Consequence? What did the World
    say?
  Hist, in the silence, to Damocles' sword!
Today Mr. Promfret has left for Karachi
  And little Miss Montague screams in her ward.

GUTTER PRESS

News Editor: Peer Confesses,
Bishop Undresses,
Torso Wrapped in Rug,
Girl Guide Throttled,
Baronet Bottled,
J.P. Goes to Jug.

But yesterday's story's
Old and hoary.
Never mind who got hurt.
No use grieving,
Let's get weaving.
What's the latest dirt?

Diplomat Spotted,
Scout Garrotted,
Thigh Discovered In Bog,
Wrecks Off Barmouth,
Sex In Yarmouth
Woman In Love With Dog,
Eminent Hostess Shoots Her Guests,
Harrogate Lovebird Builds Two Nests.

Cameraman: *Builds two nests?*
Shall I get a picture of the lovebird singing?
Shall I get a picture of her pretty little eggs?
Shall I get a picture of her babies?

86

News Editor: No!
          Go and get a picture of her legs.

          Beast Slays Beauty,
          Priest Flays Cutie,
          Cupboard Shows Tell-Tale Stain,
          Mate Drugs Purser,
          Dean Hugs Bursar,
          Mayor Binds Wife With Chain,
          Elderly Monkey Marries For Money,
          Jilted Junky Says 'I Want My Honey'.

Cameraman: *'Want my honey?'*
          Shall I get a picture of the pollen flying?
          Shall I get a picture of the golden dust?
          Shall I get a picture of a queen bee?

News Editor: No!
          Go and get a picture of her bust.

          Judge Gets Frisky,
          Nun Drinks Whisky,
          Baby Found Burnt in Cot,
          Show Girl Beaten,
          Duke Leaves Eton—

Cameraman: *Newspaper Man Gets Shot!*
          May all things clean
          And fresh and green
          Have mercy upon your soul,
          Consider yourself paid
          By the hole my bullet made—

News Editor: (*dying*) Come and get a picture of the hole.

ID

I dreamt last night
That a toad, the size of a small dog,
Swam up at me out of a city rain-butt,
Jumped to the ground and shook
Water from its empty eye-cups
And what was patchily left
Of its fur.

They said: It is in fact a dog
Who once tried to drown himself in
    the rain-butt
And found that he could not die
Under water. Go home,
They said. Go home.

But he has not gone home;
And I sit in the top storey of my house,
Wondering what else feeds in the cellar
And when I shall have to meet it.

WHO'S FOR TENNYSON?

Blow

The splendour falls from castle walls;
   We sell our only genuine Titian;
The old Duke shakes among the fakes,
   And charges five-and-six admission.
Blow, coach-horns, blow! Set the wild
     echoes flying!
Blow, coach-horns! Answer, echoes:
     'Dying, dying, dying!'

Marijuanha In The Moated Grange

With verdigris the kitchen-pots
   Were thickly covered one and all;
Her matted hair hung down in knots
   And there were gin-stains on the wall.
The open oven-door look'd strange,
   The gas came hissing from the jets,
   The ash of endless cigarettes
Littered the rusty cooking-range.
   She only said 'Would life were briefer!
   He cometh not,' she said.
She said 'I want a reefer, a reefer.
   I would that I were dead.'

EPITAPH FOR A COLUMNIST

Believing that his hate for queers
Proclaimed a love for God,
He now (of all queer things, my dears)
Lies under his first sod.

A LEADEN TREASURY
OF ENGLISH VERSE

O nuclear wind, when wilt thou blow
  That the small rain down can rain?
Christ, that my love were in my arms
  And I had my arms again.

*   *   *

Come unto these yellow sands
And then take hands;
Till bacterial cyclones blow.
Then let go.

*   *   *

I shot a missile into the air:
It fell to earth I know not where.
Since when, for some odd cause or other,
I've had no news about my brother.

Ring-a-ring o' neutrons,
A pocket full of positrons,
A fission! A fission!
We all fall down.

*   *   *

Two blind mice,
See how they run!
They each ran out of the lab with an oath,
For a small gamma ray had been aimed
   at them both.
Did ever you see such a neat little growth
On two blind mice?

*   *   *

'Mary, Mary, quite contrary,
   Say how the bomb test went.'
'I'll let you know in a week or so,
   When I've had my Happy Event.'

WEATHER FORECAST

A red sky at night
Means it went off all right.

FROM A MODERN STUDENT'S
SONG BOOK

My wife and I worked all alone
In a little lab we called our own.
Six months saw our Project flower
And we sold the result to a Foreign Power,
Ha, ha, ha! He, he, he!
Little brown bug, don't I love thee?

*   *   *

When Britain first at Heaven's command
Arose from out the azure main,
She scarce foresaw how Heaven planned
To plunge her right back in again.
Cool, Britannia! beneath the nuclear wave
While the bigger, bigger nations misbehave.

*   *   *

Bombs shall dig our sepulchre
And bigger bombs exhume us.
Gaudeamus igitur
Juvenes dum sumus.

FROM A MODERN HYMNAL

The day God gave thee, Man, is ending;
The darkness falls at thy behest,
Who spent thy little life defending
(From conquest by the East) the West.

The sun, that bids us live, is waking
Behind the cloud that bids us die,
And in the murk fresh minds are making
New plans to blow us all sky-high.

*   *   *

Hark, the herald angels sing
Glory to the newborn thing
Which, because of radiation,
Will be cared for by the nation.

*   *   *

Rock of ages cleft for me,
Let me hide myself in thee.
While the bombers thunder past,
Shelter me from burn and blast;
And though I know all men are brothers,
Let the fallout fall on others.

*   *   *

As with gladness men of old
Did the guiding star behold,
So with joy this starry night
They hail the latest satellite.
Gloria in excelsis! We
Nearer come, my God, to Thee.

*   *   *

Onward, Christian soldiers,
Each to war resigned,
With the Cross of Jesus
Vaguely kept in mind.

*   *   *

New every morning is the love
With which our Ministers approve
Devices swift and up-to-date
For fostering the same old hate.

*   *   *

The Last Noel the Angel did say
Was to certain poor people in fields as they
lay;
In fields where they lay to salve somebody's
pride:
'Noel!' said the Angel; and no one replied.

———————

THREE POEMS
From the French by Jacques Prévert

EXERCISE BOOK

Two and two four
four and four eight
eight and eight sixteen . . .
Once again! says the master
Two and two four
four and four eight
eight and eight sixteen.
But look! the lyre-bird
high on the wing
the child sees it
the child hears it
the child calls it
Save me
play with me
bird!
So the bird alights
and plays with the child
Two and two four. . . .
Once again! says the master
and the child plays
and the bird plays too. . . .
Four and four eight
eight and eight sixteen
and twice sixteen makes what?
Twice sixteen makes nothing
least of all thirty-two
anyhow
and off they go.

For the child has hidden
the bird in his desk
and all the children
hear its song
and all the children
hear the music
and eight and eight in their turn
off they go
and four and four and two and two
in their turn fade away
and one and one make neither one nor two
but one by one off they go.
And the lyre-bird sings
and the child sings
and the master shouts
When you've quite finished playing the fool!
But all the children
are listening to the music
and the walls of the classroom
quietly crumble.
The windowpanes turn
once more to sand
the ink is sea
the desk is trees
the chalk is cliffs
and the quill pen
a bird again.

II

THE HURDY-GURDY

I play the piano
said one
I play the fiddle
another
I the banjo I the harp
I the clarinet
I the bagpipe I the flute
and I the flageolet
And they all began to talk talk
talk of what they played.
Nobody heard the music
for the talk talk talk talk
talk, and nobody played
but in a corner a man sat silent:
'What do you play, good sir,' they said,
'who sit so silently
with nothing at all to say?'
'I play the hurdy-gurdy
the knife I also play,'
said the man who sat so silently
with nothing at all to say
and he advanced with knife in hand
and solemnly killed the entire band
and he played the hurdy-gurdy
and his music was so true
so pretty and so new
that the master's little girl came out
from under the piano stool
shaking a sleepy head
and said:

I played at hoop and hide-and-seek
at hopscotch too I played
and once I played with a bucket
and once I played with a spade
I played at being papa, mama,
Puss-in-the-corner and He
I played with a doll and a parasol
and whoever would play with me
I played with my little sister
I played with my little brother
I played at being a policeman
I played at being a robber
But that's all over and done done done
I want to play at murder
that's all over and done I want
to play the hurdy-gurdy
He took the little girl by the hand
and both went on ahead
through town and house and garden
and struck the people dead.
Whereafter they were wed
and they bore a great many children
but
the eldest learnt the piano
the second the violin
the third learnt the bagpipe
the fourth the clarinet
the fifth the flageolet
and they began to talk talk
talk talk and then
nobody heard the music
and all began again!

III

HOW TO PAINT THE PORTRAIT
OF A BIRD

First paint a cage
with an open door
then paint
something pretty
something simple
something fine
something useful
for the bird
next place the canvas against a tree
in a garden
in a wood
or in a forest
hide behind the tree
without speaking
without moving . . .
Sometimes the bird comes quickly
but it can also take many years
before making up its mind
Don't be discouraged
wait
wait if necessary for years
the quickness or the slowness of the coming
of the bird having no relation
to the success of the picture
When the bird comes
if it comes
observe the deepest silence

wait for the bird to enter the cage
and when it has entered
gently close the door with the paint-brush
then
one by one paint out all the bars
taking care not to touch one feather of the bird
Next make a portrait of the tree
choosing the finest of its branches
for the bird
paint also the green leaves and the freshness of the wind
dust in the sun
and the sound of the insects in the summer grass
and wait for the bird to decide to sing
If the bird does not sing
it is a bad sign
a sign that the picture is bad
but if it sings it is a good sign
a sign that you are ready to sign
so then you pluck very gently
one of the quills of the bird
and you write your name in a corner of the picture.

———————

ROMANTIC LANDSCAPE
(To Cecil and Jill Day-Lewis)

I

It is, I suppose, a picture of nowhere; or rather
Of somewhere the artist had always intended to go,
And never could find; but, fishing for colours he saw
Pooled in the iris of the mind's eye, discovered
Moss, fern, mallow, the Greek sun leaving the dale,
Reflected temples, and a blue mountain
Riding the far-off mist, its western rockface
Caught in the afterglow.

And I think that he, unquiet in the long night watches,
Hearing the crack of the rain's whip on the glass,
Is the boy under the buckthorn, watching the cattle:
Fly-hazed heifer and calf, the white and the chestnut
Hock-deep in the green water under the viaduct
Where lotus-lilies float that fail with the sun,
And Artemis watches the watcher, her marble shadow
Unmoving over the grass.

For him in Arcadia the sun stands still
As it stood in Avalon. The waterfall
Is still as the silver birch is still as the white
Corinthian columns. Neither moon nor minnow,
Rising, shall augur dusk: but under the sunlight
The boy is always a boy; the water on the weir,
The fern on the rock, the cloud in the washed sky
Stand, and are still.

105

And this I believe: that the painter cared for his landscape,
Because it was doubly dead. These moonshine temples
Lived only in the mind's eye; yet, to be loved, themselves
Had to be pictured lifeless and therefore at peace.
So the groves are empty. So the seven reeds are silent
For lack of a piping wind. Daphnis is dead,
Pan is dead, and a boy dreams in the cotton-grass
Where no hoof tramples.

This is the empty hour between one god's death
And the birth of Another; when men have looked their last
On the old disquiet and not yet turned to the new.
Now Artemis, hunting Orion for haunting the Daybreak,
Dreams herself stricken at the rising of a new Star
In the livid East. Now is the lull before
Christ stormed Maenalus—as who, in these braying days,
Shall storm the hill of Christ?

So the cattle wait to be led from the stream to the manger,
And the world waits to be led from a death to a birth,
And all I know is that under my high window,
Seven years after the truce, the neglected bombsite
Over the road is beginning to look like the picture:
Still as a valley between the shelving houses,
Quarried, pillared and ferned, already becoming
The quietest place on earth.

III

O in what far summer, when the City is rubble,
When the willowbay hangs fire on the Temple wall

And a wingless Eros halts the silently darting
Traffic of lizards in a green Circus,
Shall the scene be finally set—to recur, long after
In the backward vision of eyes at odds with the darkness,
Sifting Elysian dreams from the legendary past
Which is our present Hell?

Already, this evening, under my April window
Another cycle of the millennial myth
Coils its green spring. Surely among these children
Loitering at twilight by the static water,
Stands one in the wilderness—foreshadowing
The boy unborn who, at a far-off hour
Shall watch the altar where his brother, once,
Kicked at an upturned bath.

This, only, is certain: that a vanished landscape
Is linked with the prospect in the street below;
That when I began to write, the link was forged
In the flash of the setting sun which, once again
Flooding my window, colours the final page.
And I turn my face to the wall where, bright on the canvas,
The last light of England moves over Arcady
Two thousand years ago.